Optimism Blues:
Poems Selected and New

Michael McIrvin

Fearful Symmetry Publications

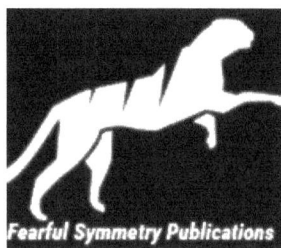

Fearful Symmetry Publications

ISBN: 978-1-7341970-5-1

Second Edition
10 9 8   7   6   5   4   3   2   1

The poems in this collection were first published in: *The Angle, The Archer, Art Word Quarterly, Bitter Oleander, Black Moon, Black River Review, Blue Mesa Review, Cedar Hill Review, The Colorado North Review, Conduit, Callapooya Collage, The Dakotah, Defined Providence, Dog River Review, Eratica, High Plains Register, Icarus Review, Icon, The Iconoclast, Intercultural Writers Review, Joe Pages Broadsides, Kaspah Raster, Loblolly, Mobius, The New Laurel Review, New Millennium Writings, The Owen Wister Review, Parting Gifts, Passages North, Phase and Cycle, The Pannus Index, Pinyon Poetry Review, Poets On, Prairie Winds, Proscenium, Pygmy Forest Broadside Series, Raw Seed Review, Redneck Review of Literature, Semi-Dwarf Review, Sierra Nevada College Review, Sulfur River Literary Review, Visions International, The Voice from Beyond, Westering, Xib.*

The poem "Father Hunger" first appeared in the anthology, *Fathers: A Collection of Poems,* edited by David and Judy Ray.

The author gratefully acknowledges the publishers of the collections that make up this book: Blue Textual Sparrow Press, Pygmy Forest Press, and Cedar Hill Publications.

Cover Art: "The Nest," by Constant Montald, reproduced by permission of the Royal Museum of Fine Arts of Belgium, Brussels.

Cover Design: Endeavor Books

First published: Cedar Hill Publications, 2003

Fearful Symmetry edition: 2020

Contents

Love and Myth

Lessons of Radical Finitude

DOG

The Book of Allegory

Optimism Blues

Necessary Errata

Love and Myth

*To be a poet in a destitute time
means: to attend, singing, to
the trace of the fugitive gods.*
Martin Heidegger

Child's Game with a Blue Balloon

A blue world:
my son's forehead, nose,
and lips crushed
against its soft outer
skin, a perfect blue navel
in his mouth. Across
the blue distance I look
back, my nose and lips
pushed tight against
blue skin too

as if this were the split
second between lifetimes,
between slipping out
of the dead blue skin of this life
and sliding into the birth-blue
skin of the next:

the soul straining, uncertain,
across the oceanic distance
to reach deep into its new home,
to take new root, the old
address a slender moment from ruin.

The Cave

We dug through short grass prairie
dirt, through the top of a low hill,
first with our hands, fingernails
turned to black crescents,
then sticks, then buckets and shovels
someone brought from home.

When the hole was three feet deep
we expanded its bottom in all directions
and dug deeper. Someone brought scrap
lumber and nails, and with a rock hammer
we built a ladder. We hauled dirt
for three days under heavy sun.

At the end of that last and hottest day
our hole led to a room ten feet across
and as many deep. We stopped work
in the late afternoon heat, knowing
without saying it was done, climbed
into the cool dark and sat in a circle
with our backs to the wall.

We looked a long time through low light
and dust, breathed the dank womb smell
of earth, listened to the slow breath
and heartbeat of the prairie, the planet,
until our mouths could not help
but hum in unison, an immense
movement to match our astonishment.

And when we emerged, still silent, into twilight,
the west horizon dripping red, we headed
our separate directions home
to late suppers and the hell we'd catch,
the world wholly changed.

Of Love and Myth

In the high strung pitch of the heart,
in the fever pitch of lips crossing flesh,
is the secret single note
that is the true sign of love's presence,
apart from biological imperative,
from shape-shifting psychological facade,
from the silly stories TV has encoded
to pull us further into the labyrinth.

The note is hidden in a hard shell
that must be cracked with the teeth,
an acrid taste like singed almonds
set loose in the mouth. Its sound
when freed is at the far range
of human hearing, a shriek
as if a lonely God made of light
and celestial wind had discovered
us and was startled into the creation of joy.

Death Dance

The seed heads of the grass
hang heavy and golden
in the last pink light of day,
and the nighthawks are flying
against a last quarter moon
                    already risen,
when out of the pink and blue
a male sharp-shinned falls
on a flock of flickers
huddled
in the certainty
of his arrival. He knocks one down
just as it leaves the ground.
The bird flaps its wind-empty wings
three times, then slowly opens
them one last time,
leans its head back
                  and does not move.
One black eye watching the hawk.
The hawk watching the eye.
All that is true suspended between them.

Mushroom Hunting on Barrett Creek

A coyote skull bleached white,
lower jaw missing, deep set
eye sockets staring blank,
the bone edges and sagittal
crest worn away exposing
the honeycomb structure
that once held marrow
and that gives a skull
its tensile strength, honey-
comb turned slightly green
from the skull's long stay
on the forest floor in dark
and duff and rain.

I imagine the rough remains
of my own head in the dirt,
a stereotypical vacancy
in these woods where no
passage means more
than any other, a perfect
construct deliquescing
where it fell, useless. I place
the mushrooms I carry,
boletus edulus, in a coyote
skull basket and carry them home.

The Tone of a Certain Reality

I want to believe
in the breast
that curves under
my callused palm,
parabola and parable,
a manifest geometry
of desire and sustenance. . .

I want to believe
in the song, exultant
and rude, that sticks
in the holy throat
of the meadowlark
on the fence post
across the road. . .

I want to believe
in my son's prayer
that our race is not
a bad joke stuttered
in an idiot's sleep,
not the amusement
of some cruel god. . .

I want to believe. . .
but every Friday
precisely at noon
the civil defense
sirens sound, a test
and a mnemonic
for our collective
nightmare drug to day-

light and given a name,
like any god, in which a man
witnesses his neighbor's
bones, his loved one's,

a split second before his own
burst into flame:

sharp C above middle C.

Guatemalan Nocturne

Disconnected hands,
like the wings of a large
flightless bird in the dust,
will no longer pound a chest
with fury, or make a guitar groan
in Latin rhythm, or caress
a lover, or clasp in prayer.

Disconnected tongues will no longer
speak, except in a voice to equal
the dust's, in the syntax of raw meat,
in the absolute monotone that is the lexicon
of death. . . and, rarely, as a benevolent
whisper in our dreams: *watch out, watch out. . . .*

But what continually amazes the executors
of torture is none of this, but that their task
does not end: more tongues and hands
to sever daily, no matter how hard they work.

Trout Fishing in America

for Richard Brautigan 1935-1984

A trout colored wind blows
through my eyes. . . .

It is early June,
the sun now two steps closer
to solstice than to equinox,
and native wisdom says
the rainbow have finished
spawning, their seed spilt
and stripes fading to mere
brilliance. But today, Billy pulled
the grandfather of all trout
out of Big Creek, lower lip
curled up over the top
and body scarred from year
upon year of corybantic
journeys. And as Bill holds
the fish up to show me
what he's caught, the trout
in his fatal gasping lets go
his silver stream of come
down Bill's arm, drops of milt
falling to the water
in the frighteningly perfect
shape of bullets to the brain.

Cooking Silence, Growing Poems

Silence, cooked like gold, in
charred
hands.
Paul Celan

You must be careful to catch
the quiet at the sharp
edges of words,
to roll it in your
burnt palm, pop it
into your mouth
and feel its weight,
its roundness
with the tongue.

You must swallow it,
feel the silence glow golden
in the belly, feel it
dissolve into your blood
and become muscle,
become bone. Feel it
fire in the synapse.
Feel it coalesce again
in the inner ear,
humming.

You must know
its sleep in the regular
rhythm of your breath
and wait patiently
for it to blossom.

Gift

I want to make
a poem of this land,
to give it to my sons
like the bread we pass,
hand to hand, over the table
of their childhood,

a poem to carry
the feminine curves,
expansive dryness, weather
that moves as God's frenetic
dreaming through tall grass,

a poem that shows
the heart-shaped prints
of deer and a badger's
eyes dark as space,
that lets loose the acute
scream of the red-tailed hawk

hovering — a poem to sift
my ashes as they scatter
through the roots, to make
a necklace of my eyeteeth
as a gift for my sons —

a poem to hold
my breath and the wind
and my sons' breathing
in a shifting and ephemeral knot
that is the song of our tremulous dancing
here.

Lessons of Radical Finitude

Lament

Whom will you cry to, heart? More and more lonely,
your path struggles on through incomprehensible
mankind. All the more futile perhaps
for keeping on toward the future,
toward what has been lost. . . .
Rilke

Mile after mile
over the glistening earth
the land is folded in white
like crystalline linen,
and milepost after milepost
I mourn the death of love,
its slow agony
through the blood-soaked
century, its final icy gasping
recorded in our breath.

The road winds black
through these hills, a scar
across the pale shoulders
of a woman who sleeps
on her belly, weeps in dreams
of men in night-colored clothing
binding her, kicking
her with steel toed boots,
carrying her away toward
the inevitable future.

A distant city's signal fades
and the radio pours only static
into the car, noise
sinister in its mechanical
whiteness. The engine hums,
vicious, monotonous. The tires
hum in yet another key.

The truth is not a simple
matter. Symbols blur, collide,

fuse in seamless mass,
and with the push of a button
the harbingers of apocalypse
smile over the airways, a song
of love on their metal lips. Brutal
and stupid, but our favorite lie.

In the Fog

The sky seethes emptiness
and across the road horses stand,
brown flanks to the silence,
heads lowered, tails
slack, like great war ponies
tired of their burdens,
the smell of blood
and unburied flesh.

Your name joins the implacable
whiteness of the air. I push
the syllables outward
toward where you sleep
at this early hour, imagine
the notes entering your ear,
soft, palpable things
to coax you awake.

The horses do not move
except to shake moisture
from their manes or to snort
fog from dappled nostrils.
A roan stallion, his muzzle
uplifted, listens to his own
heartbeat or to the movement
of the air or to remembered words
of a song to raise the sun.

You will call in an hour,
send the schedule for today,
who will take our sons *where*,
and nothing more over copper wire
and into my ear, talking
from the deep sleep that is your life
as the roan rears with all his strength
against this haze that will not lift.

Wondering What Could Be About

A Poem for, and in collaboration
with, Jesse, age four.

1

Once there was a boy who wondered
if there was a green city. He drove
a dented blue Volkswagen
looking for some sign
                                  of organic mercy.

Once, he thought he saw his parents
riding together in a limousine,
the great blue boat of connubial bliss.

2

The boy wondered if there were volcanoes
in his world. He looked, not far,
and sure enough there were.

He wondered if there was a Grand Canyon,
a monstrous scar running deep through stone.
He went to check, and sure enough there was.

He watched a little girl on her blue bike
ride through the blue streets, singing. He
watched, jealously, a plane escape

into thin air.

3

The boy dreamt every night,
in color, of dancing goats (green)
of horses (also green) that move
in lines through a distant sky.

He dreamt of another goat, singular
(this one mountain blue), who
smiled just as the boy smiled,
wept as he wept, a muscular
heave in his shoulders as tears
strained down his face,
who could not dance
for the hole in his heart.

The goat was walking
toward the sun, away,
his horned head bowed.

An American Fairy Tale

. . .sometimes you gotta do like Elvis
and shoot the damned thing out.
Bob Dylan

Elvis was an angel whose soul
flowed as a blue light from his eyes,
rolled mellifluous as honey
off his tongue. . . a cherub
who drank deep from a celestial
cup filled with proletarian
lament that mixed in his throat
with his more ordinary sadness:
for lost innocence, for the wispy
anemia of the dream.

One day a man in a smart suit
offered Elvis a bag of money to stand
in a box, to fold the blue light
from his eyes into its mechanical
light, to let it stream into American
houses and reflect off the moon-like
faces of the watchers:

So Elvis stands in a luminous circle,
intermittently but forever, with a hunch-
backed electronic father who pats him on the head
to assure him (and the watchers) that Elvis
is a good boy in spite of his angelic ass
moving to the music like a charmed
snake, shaking the father with something
akin to hunger but sadder. . . .

So Elvis sits, forever, in a circle of images,
a useless guitar on his lap, his lip twisted
into a permanent sneer, eyes raven-

black and without reflection like the dead. . .
where he speaks nonsense and the images

laugh, where he moans parodically
in an affected angel's voice.

It is rumored, somewhere in the drift
of time a man who called himself Elvis
in dark glasses and perfect pompadour,
as he sat wrapped in the folds
of his amplified flesh, emptied
a revolver into dancing shapes
on a screen, his face blank as white noise
before the final implosion
that one day sucked all air
from the room.

The Horse of Rage

The horse of rage sleeps between my shoulders.
It awakens from time to time, lifts its drowsy head,
its eyes that look through my eyes fierce to behold.
Then it sleeps again. I do not know what its dreams
are made of. The murderer who has never killed
merely sleeps the uneasy sleep of great fire
smoldering, a spark here and there to remind me:
I must ride that miserable roan one day or die under
its hooves that are made of nothing but remorse.

Working for the Union Pacific

1

We sit in the work shack
shivering in the early morning dark
waiting for the 55 gallon drum
that is our coal stove
to swallow up the cold,

waiting for the work trains
so we can buckle their iron bellies
shut with rods of steel, waiting

to push the bars into the jack's
orifice that closes the metal doors that release
the rock that lies between the tracks. . .

waiting to use my strong, 18 year old hands
I open and close to keep my fingers warm,
as my partner Julio opens and closes his hands,

horned with age and arthritis. . . waiting
with Julio who curses the weather and his God
for the pain in his shoulders, knees, loins —
his Spanish flying so fast I only catch
the swear words with any certainty. . .

and *Dios* in the same breath as *devastar*. . . .

2

Julio walks with an ache
that runs the length of his body,
which cracks when he bends
like a musical forest in the wind,
an ache so long with him
it is his being, all of what he knows.

Today, he limps and sings in Spanish
as we walk to the end of the spur
where a few work cars await us. Thirty
tons of steel at a time roll past,
gentle as cows, to join the herd
at the end of the line. We
are to reconnect the brakes.

I hook up the cars that stand quietly
while Julio waits for the next to arrive.
He rests his gloveless hand on the cold
metal hitch, watches the beast move
toward him through the gray cloud
of his breath. He shrieks as the cars couple,

blood and flesh and pulverized bone
of his ring finger the jism
in their mechanical joining. He
holds his hand up to show me his loss
and two tears fall to the ground, mix
with the red already there, a morsel
into an open mouth.

3

I kneel with the rest of the crew
in the cold belly of a boxcar, roll
the carved knuckle bones of a man
across a broken cardboard box,
bounce them off the wall shouting
siete, come *siete. . .* roll a five

and shout in pidgin Spanish, come
five. . . for quarters, for hours.

4

Julio rolls in the ground
fifteen years now, fingerless.
In my dream he dreams of trains
that never arrive, on time
or otherwise, his own hell made
of rumors of voluptuous steel. He
crosses himself. He says God
is one eyed and stupid as any machine.
He waits to be swallowed completely
by the Mother-of-Beasts, the previously
absent wife who gnaws on him now,
the shattered token of his love
a jewel in her teeth.

Lessons of Radical Finitude:
A Fugue in Four Movements

*The poet in the time of the world's
night utters the holy. In Holderlin's
language, the world's night is the holy night.*
Heidegger

1

It is the very old dream
of a woman in her dotage,
a lonely and stumbling blasphemer
hurling half-formed utterances
at the impenetrable wall
of the world's night, her body
an abacus stuck in a single
mode: subtraction. She
shouts in her delirium,
"What must I do?"

Against her will she stands naked
at the center of an endless expanse
she cannot see but feels as cold breath
on her neck; and the expanse,
also a being, bends her over and shoves
a pale, brittle cock between her thighs,
the chaos of time filling her, lodging
in her barren womb.

Her hair shimmers like phosphorus,
and the whites of her eyes become the whole
of her eyes as her gaze turns inward
toward the ghastly seed that devours.
The old woman shivers awake in a great sweat
of being, oblivious to this irony, turns
on the clock radio and cries by the vague
light of pulsing numerals, to country
songs about love.

2

It is as unfashionable as spats
to say aloud, but this *is* the voice
of the holy: an inward breath
followed by an outward: an exchange
of the element of birds for that of trees:
a beleaguered sigh, enraptured
moan, shriek of rage or terror:
the pinched and liquid flow
of this syllabary: an energy
exacted by living and spun into motion
to set the earth itself alight
with the unmapped knowledge
that roils inside us, the mediaeval
dragon full of fire to mark our way.

3

A woman's body and a man's
sink into each other as they lean
against a postmodern sky,
the luxuriant orange moon of late
winter between its deep black thighs.

"We hold back the final dazzling
apocalypse with sighs," she tells him,
the false stars floating as fear above them.
And he, "We will struggle ceaselessly
to fill our lack with this counterpoint:
your breath over my breath."

The moon lumbers through the night,
maintaining a strategic silence
the man and woman will inevitably fail
to negate. The wind will howl
as they realize there can be no sorrow
greater than theirs, and no joy.

4

Learn to close your teeth patiently
against the dark, to lie naked
entwined in the black, sleek
absence that hums, its tongue
always in your jealous ear. Learn
to suck air through your dry lips
as the fine blades of oxygen tear
at your tender flesh. Learn
to plead with the sky for mercy,
with the silence for a simple song,
any song. Learn to love the cavernous
but invisible face that lies like cold air
everywhere against you.

Telling Time

> *In the company of babies,*
> *one is very close*
> *to the kingdom of death.*
> Galway Kinnell

It is late, and my son's torso,
untouched by sunlight for months,
glows like ivory by the light of the lamp.

He is liquid on strong, short legs
as he moves across the room to search
a pile of toys in the corner.

His belly pushes out a little way
over the edge of gray sweat pants
like the smallest crescent of a pale moon,

his rib cage a ladder of vines that embrace him,
that hold the moon suspended at the margin
of thin and restful clouds. I deem

him a beautiful clock of muscle and bone
by which I tell the season, the hour
of the day — his shoulders slightly hunched,

scapula stuck out like powerful, white knives
to bifurcate this world from the next, as he prepares
to do that short forward roll into sleep.

Amazing Grace

> *. . .how sweet the sound that saved a wretch like me.*
> Traditional Hymn

> *. . .learn to forget that passionate music. It will end.*
> *True singing is a different breath, about*
> *nothing. A gust inside the god. A wind.*
> Rilke

For Sharon

In the diamond silence of night, under
the flowering sky, in the sweet breath
of ten thousand wild plum blossoms,
I am pissing on the pitch-black earth
and humming slow and soft to the hymn
you wrap around me from behind like arms,
that you send through me, the words
entering just under my right scapula to swim
through my chest and resonate in my throat
as cold creek water, your words
that rise like trout barely breaking the surface
before descending back into the deep,
the elemental flow that is their being.
In this moonless mountain night your song
holds my body as a cocoon, mates
with silence within me, and briefly
I am the absolute joy of living
and of death.

DOG

Sniffing the trees,
just another dog,
among a lot of dogs. What
else is there? And to do?
Only the lame stands—on
three legs. Scratch front and back.
Deceive and eat. Dig
a musty bone. . . .

Prelude

It is the parable of a charred future
that shimmers just beyond us
against the empty field of invisible
distance, the dialectical fulcrum
between renaissance and ruin. From here
all signs point to this dead end,
end of the street, the century, of obscene
time and its breath of putrid history. . .
or else toward what?

In one hand the parable teller
holds horror and sacerdotal being,
balanced, holds outcry and praise
copulating wildly. In his other
hand is stasis, death: a blind
and contorted pup who would be admonition
if it were not already too late.

The singer himself is lame: the hand
that holds the blind dog shriveled,
his voice small and incidental as rubble,
a broken tool, a bent weapon. He
is drunk with fear. It sleeps, nameless,
in his liver.

He shifts from one foot
to the other on the smoldering plain
that holds the smoky stench
of death itself like a rising demiurge;
but also knowledge, ten-thousand gods,
dancing, song. . . and the bodies
that have melted to rings of bone,
puddles of coagulated gore: testimony
to a terror that is species-specific.

The parable teller shakes like St. Vitus
and whimpers until the plain echoes.
Then there is a shriek, a roar

that aspires to be living wind, aspires
to sweep the field clean: *a new start,*
a new start, a new start. . . . The parable
teller fails. He must settle for his own
brutal song, for the field only slightly,
but irrevocably, changed.

Dog on Fire

Dog walks on his hind legs,
as in an old joke, into a run-down bar,
head of a dehorned goat over the door,
at the end of the street, end
of the twentieth century. He orders
a double shot of hot redemption
and cold beer chaser like a movie
cowboy, like James Bond, throws
both back, slams his fist on the bar,
like Pizarro, like Christopher Columbus
unzipping his pants in the New World,
the third world.

Pain in his one good hand
reminds him of reckless desire,
soft hair on the nape of the last cur
he held hard as iron, threw
to the ground and rode toward
the homeland of release
for all he was worth.

Debatable assertion, worth,
thinks Dog as the worm of redemption
warms his frontal lobe. Stops
him cold. A paradox, thinks Dog,
to run hot and cold at the same time,
to be wolf-cousin and lap-sitter,
howler and whiner, kisser
of hands, pisser-on-everything-
to-own-it, tracker, stupid chewer
of shoes, moon gazer, rabid-
humper-of-stray-legs, lone wolf,
pack follower, trickster-thief, fool-
who-drools, noble sled puller,
roller in fresh shit for no reason,

chicken killer, eater-of-grass-when-sick. . .
and friend: first and foremost,

Dog says aloud. I'm a loyal
son-of-a-bitch, he tells the bartender,
one-eyed Bob, who fills his glass.
I serve, he says, as the barman
walks away, his good eye blinking
madly, whoever feeds me, gives to me
in some measure. Trades
with me: money for time. And I
kill for master if he asks, rip
the throat out of any son-of-a-bitch
who doesn't play by the rules: heel,
sit, beg, shuffle and plead, play
dead unto barely breathing. . . .

Dog's voice trails to nothing
and he stares at the small glass
of amber, feels its boney fingers
poking at his spirit-deep sickness,
pulling at the old scab in the back
of his throat. Bile
of the question of worth
rises. His stomach rumbles,
brain smolders like a decaying
flower on its small stem, churns.
Then all quiets.

Silence, not the womb of words
but their utter absence, blazes. Cows
that won't be chased home, birds
that flush but don't sing. Coyote
with chronic laryngitis: can't praise
the moon so stops looking up,
can't say *here I am* across vacant
miles so stares at his feet
and spits like any idiot.

Dog, entombed in silence,
watches circles made by glasses
on the bar. Wet holes
in the momentarily solid world.
Emptiness overlapping. Blanks

that glisten like old stars
in low bar light. Insubstantial.
Meaningless. One-eyed Bob
brings another shot and chaser
without being asked. Strange word,
meaningless, says Dog. . . .

Dog and the Virtual Real

The new barmaid is bleeding,
thankful business is slow, tired
to her soul. She tells Dog,
through lips pale in any light,
that between her period and holes
in her stomach she can barely stand.

She says, someday, if we are lucky
there will be a machine
into which we are downloaded,
spirit exploding over the logarithmic
dream-grid, as the wound, this body
falls aside like a rag.

   She says, the race will slide
through speed jungles of wire, diodes,
capacitors, as synthesized orgasmic
flashes in cybernetic void, energy
arrows rocketing through what passes
for sky in the value-free field-heart
of the machine.

   She, this woman whose name
Dog does not know, wanders to the end
of the bar to take one more blind man's order.
Her chest heaves, a frightened animal
in her over-tight uniform cut to show
cleavage like glacial crevasse, dangerous
and tempting. Dog aches at the thought
of a slow descent into that deep cut in snow.

   But it passes. At Dog's end
of the bar hangs his nightmare given form
in an anonymous shamaness' vision
of overburdened being, of our weary selves

encoded, alternating current, yin and yang
boiled to electric purity. Abdication

of the animal at light speed. Benevolent
addiction in a bottomless digital box.

      Maybe, thinks Dog, flesh has become
anachronism, its silly selfish demands at last
more than we can stand. No eating,
fucking, or dreams rising out of frosted
libidinous ponds. Might be a blessing.
No lament rocked slow over the plain
of desire. No dancer, but pulsating
particles dancing by goblin light.

      Maybe to evolve is to dissolve
to shifting punk strands of energy
within what we have made. Maybe
to pray is to transubstantiate to uncritical
waves, bouncing. Maybe, frequency
and velocity are transcendent essence of need.
An ice cube explodes in a blind man's glass
at the far end of the bar, throws
amber sparks toward the sky
like a holy man's gift.

Maybe, Dog says to the Barmaid
when she returns, hands shaking in anemic
air, body quaking in crinoline and spike heels,
in the end we will say we did not deserve
so tender a form as this one that speaks,
bleeds by power of the moon, this vessel
made of hunger, meat boat shuddering
on the surf of longing. . .

this grief that plods through American air
thick with unrecognized despair, chaser
after delinquent gods to heal us, sorrowful
soma, fist of want, useless sound cavity

yielding rattle and tap of nonsense to the wind.
Maybe we will say, if only the verb "to act"
had been more true at the end of the street,
end of the twentieth century.

Dog and the Myth of Eternal Return

My mother dreamt she carried a ghost
inside her, Dog tells the barmaid as he sways
on his seat as to music. . . an apparition
nestled inside the pouch of her stomach.

She said the ghost smelled half wild,
that it mumbled things to her, sighed,
then something in it died. Dog leans, grabs
at the bar top with both hands.

You need a ride says the waitress.
It's simple bar math: you cease
to make sense, sway and dance, and I call a cab.
Dog says, my mom was raped by my dad.

It's part of the legacy. My grandmother,
mostly Sioux, part Cree, part Navajo,
was raped by my father's father too.
A last conspicuous colonial act. 1914. South Dakota.

The barmaid dials the phone, her face
swimming before Dog in a sea of clinking glass.
Their spawn was a drunk with hands of stone,
my father. Neither Caucasian nor Indian.

He begat me upon my mother, forced
his angry seed into her to make another
with one hand of stone and the other
of meek flesh, a broken creature born

of broken creatures. Dog belches, strains
harder to stay still. But my grandmother danced
until the day she died, swayed, shook rattles
and sang. She danced for all life,

she told me. When I close my eyes,
I see her against my will, swirling

with her eyes closed, wrinkled
like nobody on earth, like earth itself.

Her face all canyons, arroyos, pocked
brown plains in the sun. The taxi
driver takes enough money from the bar
for the ride, stuffs

the remaining bills in Dog's shirt pocket,
and helps him to the door. Let
go the ghost of my mother's womb,
Dog mumbles, and I will sing to you. . .
                because the birds of meaning have flown.

            □

The birds of meaning have flown
forever south, and the myth of eternal return
died, says Dog from the cab's back seat
to the driver who pretends he has no ears.
All that remain are wing-clipped chickens,
domestic turkeys on low limbs. . .
all roosters become rooted, as flight
is tamed out of them, as wings tighten
and shorten with each generation
until even the notion of sky fades
and the immediate dirt in the shade
of their own bulk is all they know to say.
Shut up, says the driver,
and Dog falls asleep as the taxi careens
like a split atom through traffic. In a dream

Dog peers south waiting for the return
of meaning, for soarers with bright wings
pounding over the edge of earth — honking,
screeching, demanding, pleading. But

the sky remains a blank page, beautiful
blue, vacant of any sign. In his dream
Dog knows what he has always known:
the wheel of the word is broken

and the singers will never again land
on this land.

□

The pavement is cold against
his hairy cheek when Dog wakes
in front of the scar
that is the building where he lives.

He cranes his neck upward
from the stoop in the crisp air
to see Orion still stiff,
still hunting.

Dog falls up urine soaked
stairs that creak, past
doors where the anonymous
sleep, snore, weep.

Inside his own black door
Dog falls onto his bed.
His grandmother's voice
echoes through dream:

Once, she says, a snow-blinded
maiden wandered lost over
the high plains, stumbled,
crawled, slept as prelude to death.

But she felt, as in a dream,
the pelt of God in her hand
and was awakened by a cavernous
silence and the smell of blood.

A white wolf with red eyes
stared at her, nodded solemn
as stone at a dead rabbit
on the altar of her bare breasts.

She fainted with fear.
She thought the rabbit's eyes
were the eyes of death, that death
sat upon her chest to gnaw her spirit.

When she awoke the wolf
was gone, and she ate the rabbit
raw, drank snow melted in her hands,
and slept again.

The wolf returned. She sat
up as he bowed to her, licked
her everywhere. She turned
her bare ass to him and he mounted.

The fury of that act made
the maiden howl, her eyes glow
red, her flesh quiver. Warmth
of his semen made her sigh.

She returned to the people
a wild queen dressed in white
buckskin, her hair like snow.
She told us stories, taught us to dance.

To dance. Desire is our teacher,
she said, flaming engine in the blood
that drives us. . . our noses
to the ground and lifted to the wind

to find the scent of what is true,
to follow it, relentlessly,
to discover the scat, to eat it
and grow wise, to hunt forever.

Dog's grandmother's face fades
and is replaced by a faceless
mongrel half buried in snow, back
of his brain solid stone under

a dangerous sky moving as in a film
run five times too fast.

Dog wants to run, in dream,
from his bed, but is frozen
as a corpse to his sheets
as the bloody mongrel rises,
turns slowly to feathers
and sinew: a Canada goose
big as a man. . .

stretching his wings wide
against the storm that moves
behind his beaked head, his
animal erection aimed at the moon.
The bird squawks once, whips
its wings to wind, and is gone.

Dog Sings the Shotgun Blues

We wandered together to the edge of earth
where iron-fisted fires of grief
rule. I stopped, afraid. You leapt
through the blaze into space in the posture
of prayer, into invisible arms
to release your mind, you said, frozen
numb for all the loss. To squeeze
your form to pieces and send nameless
fragments of carcass into the void beyond
our meager understanding.

In this very room where I drink alone,
you knelt before my one black window
you proclaimed a doorway, laid
the smooth, night-blue barrel
on your tongue, and pushed all the words
you have used in your life backward

                                        as flame.

The crown of your head came off
like a portal, pieces of you everywhere.
Your final erection sprouted toward
the sky, a last desire blossom
pointing outward, toward union,
as you bled. I wailed at the sight
of my beloved brother's blood, drove
claws into my good palm until I bled
with you as I looked into your brain
like the entrails spread for a diviner.

I saw only the silence of corpuscles
and meat blazing; and fear bloomed in me,
became the awful fruit full of ripe seed
I sow daily, germ of future poisonous
harvests to keep the generations aphasiac

as my own. I no longer howl for the dead,
that single high note of praise

and pain my grandmother taught me.
I answer the daily indiscriminate massacre
with a stillness to equal death's own hush,
with the murderous quiet of a frightened witness.

My friend, today I am drunk
in your honor. But for courage,
I too would change my name
to *Nothing,* to *Absence,* to *Blank-wind.*
But *Soundless-space-in-clothes*
will have to do, *Voiceless-*
bag-of-hair-on-three-legs. . . .
I toast your namelessness,
for he who has no name has no wish,
and I can no longer muster words
to hold even the thinnest desire.

Dog and the Dream of the Unwashed Self

For days Dog has seen only shotgun
splatter in his dreams, smelled
sulfur and blood, heard lead
fly slow motion through the air,
a prayer played backward,
become evil incantation, dragging
Dog by his hair toward his body's
                                own conclusion.

Right now he hears a shotgun's single
note, abrupt, held a split second,
repeated over and over, the sound
of one hand, chant of despair, dirge
for a friend whose face he cannot
see for the gaping hole in the wall
of his memory, can't see for guilt.

His faceless visitor fades,
as every night, with the noise
of Dog's upstairs neighbor closing
the door, throwing her shoes
into a corner. She sleeps all day
and fucks for pay in cheap hotel rooms
all night. Foreign businessmen tie her
to chairs. Drug dealers nuzzle
her breasts like children.

Or so Dog imagines:
she is their mother confessor,
scapegoat, swallower of their effluvial
sins. . . but she hates them all,
is the dreamer-of-the-twisting-knife,
longer-after-the-death-that-lingers
for those who have stolen her life
and replaced it with fishnet stockings
                                and jism.

Dog knows her name is Camille,
a hurricane in spike heels, skirt
hitched high above a girl's
knobby knees, just below her paper-
thin ass that makes him ache with want,
makes him sad beyond words. Through
his drowsy mind now pass her sequined
purse slapping at her thigh, her tiny
breasts, black skin, fleshy lips,
brown eyes, her French braid draped
over her shoulder like a snake.

Dog sits in deep forest
crying for a vision
as his grandmother taught him,
hands of clay outstretched
over the earth in the smoke
haze of the ruins, bleeding
ravines in his palms turned
                              skyward.

Camille, handmaiden to no one,
dances like a water snake
in its death throes through a small
clearing. Her austere rags flow
in the frenetic wind of her movements
exposing the great knots

of her knees, her fish-
belly smooth thighs, her forbidding
sex that makes Dog shiver. The
bottoms of her bare feet are dark
with dirt. Your desire begins here,
she says as she points to the ground.

Dog feels fire rise through the exhausted
earth, through the chakra just above

his asshole and up his spine until all
his being burns with one flame. With
the last of his energy he stands, stumbles
                              to Camille.

He touches her hand, his blood
smearing her palm, her breast. She
runs her hands over his dusty limbs,
blows hot and mysterious breath
into his face. They dance closer

as the birds sing over them,
as Dog's heart splits like an atom
thrown around a wheel and slammed
into another atom where it spins
at the speed of light. As they dance
                              they revise

the world. Politics of sex falls away
to something purer, love redefined
as an explosion of being, a syntactic
free-for-all of flesh, the transcribed
force rising as lightning from dirt

through the soles of the feet,
the sphincter, and written on the air. We
send our spark through the silence,
says Dog, activate it with this single
collision of souls in space, give life
to what was dead. . . and as he speaks
                              in his dream

Dog and Camille push into each other,
unlock the steep sacrificial blue
that has smoldered a century or more,
and transmit the chaotically rhythmic flashes
of their dance through the newly electrified field
                              of the world.

Dog and the Burning World

The first warped shafts of daylight,
like arrows of a thousand sorrows,
or some such archaic, admonition,
huff and puff through Dog's window
where he sleeps but cannot forget.

Ghost of his grandmother, whose
violated seed was Dog's father,
hovers at the foot of the bed. She
says, disintegration of the world
strolls with you my pup, stalks
you not ten steps behind, double-
barreled beady eyes forever aimed
                                    at your head.

Dog awakens shivering with the shock
of her voice more real than ever. At
the end of his bed Dog's grandmother's
form flickers but does not fade. Why
don't you swim back to void, old one?

What do you want from me? The
apparition begins to chant, to swing
her small, diaphanous hands outward.
Sparks arc between them, explode
as inverse lightning toward space.

Dog is certain he will die in the hail
of fire, feels the heat sear hair
from his cheekbones, feels his vocal
chords warp and quiver on the edge
of voice. He clutches the wound of his lips.

The old woman's voice soars to a single
shrill note, whether of grief or praise Dog

knows he is too much dumb animal to guess.
His hackles stand and sizzle under
hot rain. I am mortal, he says

through his fingers, no dancer
in the smoke, no morning glory blossom
in buckskin shaking rattles over the earth,
slamming my head against the sun, *just*
mortal, and bleeding from every orifice.

What can I sing, Grandmother,
in this singularly sick moment? Of the kiss
that devours? Bayonets and rockets? Fear
and the dullness in human eyes as men
and women stumble like prisoners
through their tiny spot of time?

Of their necrophilious love for the mechanical?
Their terminal desire to become the machine? How
can I erect towers of air to say: children
are tortured here in the name of belief, raped
before their mother's eyes, forced to watch

the murder of their fathers, then slaughtered too,
so that their last vision on earth is hell
and the demons who rule, of diminished
simians self-assured of their place in heaven
at the right hand or left hand or in the lap

of a God with blood in his teeth, a vision
of the dog-soldiers of dystopia marching
to the final sea at the end of time? How
can I sing the savagery of God?
How do I offer ceremonies of dust and air

to those who survive to return the favor,
to rape and torture the small and blameless,
to move us one step closer to the dark water
where history pours finally into the waves
of oblivion? No, I must look away, Grandmother,
or at least look with eyes of glass

like the rest that only reflect the world
back on its nightmaring self. The old woman's
one note stops. The shower of sparks ends
and her form wavers in advancing daylight.

The world's night, she says, demands
desire beyond this whimpering. If you
want until your heart fuses to the sky,
your backbone to the earth, until God
bellows from the hollow drum of your chest,

God whose breath is wind laid over
the electric silence of the universe dreaming,
you will have no choice but to sing, to speak,
to dream. And don't tell me no one listens.
It is beside the point. Rise from the dead, Dog,

and carry your blazing heart into the blazing
world. Worms will suck your rotting carcass
soon enough. Wake up! Dog's grandmother's
form fades to light and he rises, tired
to his core, to search for his pants.

Dog Hunts God. . .

mostly at night, always
in the street where prostitutes
and junkies meet for their sad
exchange of money: one
for her oblivious flesh, the other
for a fleshless oblivion.

Dog carries tequila in a brown
bag on the cold trail to share
with them, asks them the question
to which they all have an answer.

Tonight he offers a tall bleached
blonde his bottle. She takes a long
pull, shudders, giggles like the girl
she was somewhere in the buzz of time.

Her face is fine as hammered steel,
but her beauty is sullen, tuberculin,
thin and sharp as razor blades in Halloween
candy. Needle mark stigmata glow

pain red between her thumb and forefinger,
and Dog smells decay under her skin
that sizzles and crackles as she speaks. Sometimes
I dream, she says, of macrobiotic angels

wearing tennis bracelets and clean sneakers,
diamonds big as knuckles. At dawn
they take my hand, kiss me and give me
shining things, invite me to fly with them

to heaven. . . . A black car with chrome wheels
honks at the curb, idles nervously by street light,
the driver anonymous behind darkened windows.
Duty calls, she says, and kisses Dog's hairy cheek.

Dog tips the bottle up as the car door slams.
The smell of her perfume still burns
in his nostrils like smoldering garbage,
like meat rotting, like sorrow grown to fill

all space inside its husk of skin, enough
for an entire race. Dog watches the street
from his seat on the curb: cars the color
of murder drive by slowly, hookers

preen and pose, money and needles pass
hand to hand. A pair of long black legs
above stiletto heels stops next to Dog. A tenor
voice that longs to be alto, soprano, says,

Can I have a sip o' yo' juice big boy? Dog
hands the bottle up to the black drag queen
who could pass for a woman, except for a good
sized Adam's apple and mechanic's knuckles.

I heard the question you asked that tart. You
hunt God, huh? For the rest o' that bottle
I'll tell you 'bout God. He stands
with one hand on his hip, a coquettish man

in mini-skirt, loose silk blouse, black wig.
He waves the bottle in front of him in an arc
that takes in the street: two winos push each other,
buildings crumble like bad teeth, a prostitute

slides into a cop's cruiser. Somewhere, here,
God walks among us. . . lonely, hermaphroditic,
desirous, but embarrassed by what we have become,
by the sad slap-hands, you know, money. In

the beginning, God took himself in his own fist,
and jism of us spewed over the earth. God,
the Great Chaste Monkey, broke open his jars
of infinite semen, dispersed being, multiplied

all appearances until we became mirrors
looking into endless mirrors. But He
also multiplied death. The effort turned
Him hollow, to a husk without breath,

an emptiness that stumbles among us,
silent and grieving. The black queen tilts
the bottle up in its brown skirt, drains
it and throws it into the street where it smashes

to a million shards of light, a tiny muffled
violence no one notices. God mourns,
shouts the queen as he walks away, that this is all
senseless gesticulation. The world and the soul

have become separate things, but mirror
images, grotesque, foul. Nothing sings here.
Except, maybe, rarely, lovers. The man
who would be woman turns to look at Dog

from the corner, sways tipsy in the buzzing neon
of a bar sign. Drunk, he cannot contain his masculine
side. He shouts louder, one hand on his heart,
the other upraised: But beware the bite that drives

you at the center of your being. Both love and death
are drawn to its succulent yellow core, to the swarm,
violent and irremediable, that lives there, God's
own teeth marks still visible where he gnawed
your soul out of darkness and silence and into existence.

Take heeeeeed, big boy! Dog watches the queen
shuffle across the street as awkward as any man
in high heels, watches him lean on the hood
of a cab stopped at the light, slap the sheet metal
like a drum and grin, for all he is worth.

Dog and the Tigers of Wrath

The tygers of wrath are wiser than the horses of instruction.
William Blake

We been looking for you,
says the man in black bandanna
as he sits down on the barstool
to Dog's right, as the mirror image
of him sits to Dog's left.

Dog smells the river of their hunger
as it thunders into the ocean
of their rage. He knows they smell
his fear. I hear on the street

you're on the trail of God, been
asking everyone you meet. I'm
here to set you straight. Dog
looks out of the corner of his eye,

fumbles with his half-empty glass.
Gangbangers do not believe, says the man.
We bleed. But I am obsessed with belief
just the same. The bartender

brings both men a beer. The one
who speaks reaches into Dog's singles
on the bar to pay. He says, I have seen
children on their knees in doorways,

crying and mumbling the names of heaven
as we drive by. I have seen old men cross
themselves furiously, then curse us to hell
as we level guns at their gray heads.

I have heard a man scream, ecstatically,
"Oh my God," as his entrails slipped
through his fingers to a liquor store floor,

as if death were like coming, a last
massive orgasm of blood and organs
spewed over the ground. Hear this, man.
We are the hand of God in the absence

of God. Random as flood. Violent
as earthquake. He turns his eyes, hard
and black as revolvers, on Dog.
This trail is cold. You want to believe

in something, join us. Close to God
you gonna get is fear, then acceptance
of your own death, and joy in the deaths
of others, that their death is not yours.

Dog summons all his courage. Why
do you tell me this, he asks, his voice trembling?
We are in a holy war of sorts, says the man,
a struggle for ground and identity. We need

a priest, someone to bless the warriors,
to bury the dead. I am a gimp and a drunk,
says Dog. Not a holy man, barely a man.
His voice, no longer trembling, trails to silence.

The men in bandannas rise. That is the point,
Dog. When a Mac 10 barks in my hand,
sacred sparks flying from its rude mouth,
neither am I. . . not holy, not a man. Neither

am I animal, but an extension of the machine
in my hand and I am praying to the only things
of worth left on this planet: power and survival.
Think about it, Dog. As priest you can touch

power by touching death. You'll know you still breathe
because you too will extend the machine, because
you lay hands on the cold flesh of your comrades who
bless you with the knowledge that you are alive

as you commend them to the earth, that you
are among the not-dead. Why me, asks Dog?
Because you are a hunter, even if the trail
is long cold. The rest have the glazed eyes of prey.

☐

Dog is tired to his core as the gangbangers
walk away. His chin rests on his chest,
but he dares not close his eyes. From down
the bar a man's voice whines with an actor's diction:

What was it Blake said? "I must create
a system or be enslaved by another man's."
But what does that mean, his companion
asks, now, at the butt end of this dreary century?

Both men wear ties like pet snakes, knots
loosened, nooses about to be pulled taut.
What was it Prof. Darden said before he hung
himself, says the first speaker as he raises

his glass dramatically? "I am drowning in the dead
sea of late civilization, my self swallowed, taken
into the general wrack." The speaker laughs. His
companion doesn't. He says: Darden was right.

An endless waterfall of sanctioned images pours
over us, daily baptism unto death. It is a drug
hidden in the frosted flakes, subtext in the news,
the gist of all TV — different is dangerous.

So we grow up to be policemen, talk show hosts,
professors. . . and demand sameness too. He
is tipsy and sways on his seat. You're too serious
my young friend. What is it to be a man,

the young one asks? Impossible to say in this tumult,
this blather? To have a voice at all when you are in the choir,

confused contralto among confused contraltos? But
maybe civilization, the body politic as hygienic sameness,
is now protagonist, hero and anti-, and all words infinitesimal
testimony to power that will stay power forever and ever, amen.

Odes to the subsumed. . . . You are drunk, says the older,
tired from the work the department expects, the load
you bear. Yes, says the younger. Perhaps that is it. I
told you this seedy place has plenty of darkness,

says the older, an air of angst, an ambiance of death
that would amuse you. I think Hemingway drank here
when the neighborhood was still Irish, or Italian, probably
what killed him. Yes, says the younger. Must be the place.

When Dog's head clears he shuffles through the door
of the bar and into the night that is a blossom of exhaust
and stale urine. He nearly slams into the young professor
and the previously silent gangbanger where they talk

on the sidewalk. They are before him, but one to the left
and one to his right like cartoon angels who sit at each shoulder.
They jump through hoops, says the prof. Silly trained dogs
panting and prancing, proud of their new trick, wanting

to lick this very hand. He flexes his fingers, his palm outward.
See, nothing here, I say. Take it in your hand, or bite it
to bone, chop it off, stick it in your pants, something. . . . Smash
through constrained circles of cant, rage, breathe fire, I say

as they wag their tails and smile like a hypnotist's patients,
their tongues lolling. The banger laughs. Dog hears despair
and ridicule nesting like birds in his voice. A single silver
incisor shines in the neon. His dark glasses reflect the professor's

distorted face. I seen a man once, he says. His tongue hung down
to his chin as he stumbled over a loop of his own intestines. He

pointed his gun at the fuck who shot him, pulled
the trigger until there wasn't no more bang, then fell over.
That's the way to go, man. That's the way to be. . .
like a wolf someone wants to keep on a too short chain.

The professor's face is flushed, pink in the raging neon,
his eyes wide with incomprehension. You can't jump
through no hoops, says the banger, if you're dead.
And there ain't no hoops at all when you're the man

with the machine in your hand. A car's tires squeal
from the street like a child screaming. Flames
fly from the window. Dog falls to the ground
at the first sound. The professor does not move.

The tiger pulls a pistol from under his shirt
and throws flame-blue flowers back at the car.
Dog feels a warm sea under him, the cold sidewalk
against his cheek. The tiger curses. The young
 professor is silent.

Dog's last waking vision is of spent casings
smoking on the concrete as if they breathed
on the cool air, as if they slept now, lovers,
after violent and boisterous sex.

Dog's Resurrection

He exits through an invisible door
between his eyes, hangs above
the street where he fell in the protocol

of established absence, a shadow
with options on the cusp of unbounded
dark watching the caster-off-of-the-shadow

melt into the concrete as in an atomic
holocaust photo: the figure wedded
forever to earth by violent light.

He can see the young professor's eyes roll
backward into the oblivious heaven hidden
somewhere in the tabernacle of his skull.

He can hear the gangbanger repeating,
Oh my God, endlessly, as if he were a saint
enraptured. . . holy, holy, holy. . .

as if death were a last
massive orgasm on the void,
as the gangbanger's entrails

seep around his fingers
for some diviner of these mad streets
to read: horror, hunger, and infinite silence,

the diviner will sing, *miraculous*
distortion of human radiance. . .
but no one will listen.

Dog's spirit is sad
and he longs to cry out
that the only beauty left us

is our own blood-blossoms
in purple-red bouquets
on the sidewalk, our

own feared mortality
as it seeps somehow, inevitably,
back into the earth. . .

but the dead have no voice.
The gangster crosses himself
with his free hand,

reaches instinctively to touch
the professor's cold fingers
in their empty gesture of benediction, and is gone.

Sirens wail and Dog struggles
to wail too, at the desperate moon
where it sails invisible above neon vapor:

for frivolous flesh become dirt,
for hungry ghosts, the barely breathing
who cannot fathom what they lose

when they cease to move altogether,
for his rapist father and victim mother,
for his grandmother, her long braids hung

over her bare breasts as she sang
to him in his childhood, for the prostitute
whose apartment is above his own, for his friend dead

by his own hand. A man Dog does not know
takes his wallet, then the professor's.
He does not touch the gangster,

his bloody mess. Dog wants
to send sound waves of blessing
over the man as he runs

into the night, retching, longs
to remember his grandmother's
blessing song, but can't.

Another man Dog does not know
rolls his bleeding body over
and beats on Dog's chest.

Dog rumbles back through the door
between his eyes on a wave of sorrow,
still struggling to howl

at the moon he can't see. All
he can manage is a moan as he submerges
into the wine-dark sea of his pain,

then a splutter as blood
exits his lungs, then
thank you, as this man too

turns for the dark at a run,
as the ambulance screams to a halt,
its lights washing the whole world red.

Dog's Apocrypha

1

Dog, heedless of irony
dictates to the air: I
have no words. Voice
itself is a burden I carry
in my throat as the tubes
pass through, as I lie
on the terrible white field
of over-bleached hospital
sheets, as skin of my chest
tingles under impeccable
catgut stitches that hold
me together, body to soul.

Where in this mournful
mortal dream can I find
language to equal resurrection?
This pain — to breathe, roll
over, to bark at a comesome
nurse whose hands rouse
me to desire even as it hurts
to breathe — is precious
beyond anything else of earth.
Dog chokes on his tubes,
on his last utterance, struggles
to sit so he can stare out the window.

A flock of pigeons flies
mad through low-careening-
jet noise, surges and shifts
in a hungry line as a little
China girl stumbles toward home
through the concrete labyrinth,
unperturbed in her Catholic
uniform under the inalienable sun.
This is the picture Dog's

hospital window frames: terror,
wonder, beauty, and death written
together at once on the sky

and spilled over the daily world.
It is a small slice of the real,
but Dog quails at its sheer volume,
struggles to will himself away
from the scene, but can't.
He can't not look. The girl
lifts her eyes from the curb
she walks like a tightrope,
her arms outstretched
like a soaring, wobbling
bird. She smiles and waves
in Dog's direction, loses

her balance and steps
into the gutter as the murderous
traffic caroms by, as Dog
steps off with her and gasps,
clasps her hand with his mind
to help her back up the genteel
curb, back onto the tightrope,
to safety. Car horns wail
at her as she steps from the river
of certain death, but the child
continues as if the world
were unchanged. Dog's breath

goes hard. He feels faint, weaker
than ever in his life, lays
back and would sleep
except for the trembling,
except for the angel of fear
in whose black arms he shivers
like a child. He struggles
to imagine freedom, courage,
manhood. . . . He fails.

▢

Hours later Dog sleeps in the shallow
pond of personal, ghastly enlightenment,
in the room where women's hands spin
the warp and woof of survival
from murder and the matted, bloody
hair of angels amid the animal
cries of our general suffering. He
fears he will drown there,
in what he knows.

Dog slips into dreams of a dancer
in scarlet turning, her knobby knees
and scrawny ass signs of her youth.
Camille, hurricane whore whose room
is above Dog's rented room. He
dreams the guitar of love strums
the effulgent song of her body, his voice
springing outward as praise; he dreams
his voice becomes hands that caress

her scarlet curves, translate her
to vapor and sunlight, to purpose,
as if the agonized night, the morphine,
thorazine night where sleep
and the waking self coalesce,
were not itself but the obverse/reverse,
darkest night's sparkling mirror image:
Joyous-day-like-the-steps-of God-
through-clouds, as in a painting
made when humans were still capable
of such a vision.

▢

On the feminine side of midnight
Dog is wrapped in a sparrow's wing,
in the speckled dark that breaks
over him as an ocean of appetite,
but also in all the voices of his past

that fold around him like fingers
around a throat. His dream
of Camille gives way to nightmare:
that the universe has teeth
and is hungry for his soul.

Dog's fish-white belly heaves.
His soul is a frightened animal
raging to escape, to fly
into the chiaroscuro of his hospital
room, to merge with the color
of iron, dead branches, soot covered
snow, the color of an old man's withered
flesh that emanates from the surface
of everything at this hour.

Then, suddenly, he is calm.
Death has rattled Dog,
a gourd of innards and gangbanger's
bullets that beat him nearly blind.
He click-clacks now as he stares
from his bed at the black ceiling
that has become the dark maw of the shaker-
of-gourds, become a black gate of seething
nothing palpable as heartbeat, more.

The shaker's tongue lunges into his ear
pulling up small hard seeds of despair
and replacing them with the singer's
wind, filling Dog with hot balls
of gaseous desire, churning.

2

Camille looks at Dog with Billie
Holiday's 1957 eyes, filled
to the brim with a terminal blues. She
stares in his direction as at the blank
stone wall of the future.

Dog moans to Camille where she sits
on the bed, her back propped
against the corner of the room,
her bare legs spread.

You have awakened me from a dream
of self-immolation where flames
turn to words that flow from me
hot as fire, the smell of my flesh
burning given up as smoke offering to heaven.

You have awakened me to passion,
to your body's dreaming
that denies you sleep, and I
am ecstasy. Splendor,

he sings, rhapsodic, thy name
is woman. . . . Fuck you Dog,
says Camille, her voice a plain,
a sheet of glass. A woman

who screws all night for money
does not "make love" lightly,
but I was awake and lonely
and the only way to rouse you

was to wake your dick. Dog
raises up on one elbow. . .
but I love you, he says.
Camille laughs. So you want

to do that old duet of depravity,
play incubus to my succubus?
She points to her bare labia:
Is this a gift I give you

or commodity, what I trade
for your momentary comfort. . .
or is it your temporary stay
against terror, the knowledge

your life is a tiny wave
in the dark and horrific sea
of history? Maybe, says Dog,
love is our attempt to merge

with the disembodied body
of some larger text, to step
into human being if only
for a split second. Camille

grimaces. Love is violence Dog,
she says, at least violent sequestration
as some old professor told me
as we took turns being tied to the bed. . . .

So I am the same as a customer,
asks Dog? No, says Camille,
and pats his bare, wire-haired thigh.
You don't pay me. Besides,

we are all sold continually
into slavery. My whoredom
is merely metaphor made manifest.
Why am I here, asks Dog,

tears welling embarrassingly.
This is as close to love as we
are allowed Dog: no money and as minimal
violence as humans are capable,

the sloppy slap of flesh
pushed hard to flesh.

Dog's illusions die in the gray air
of his room as Camille dresses:
I had wanted this want, he says,
to be translated to tender purpose,
a reason to breathe.

Camille pulls her silken hose up
her thighs, over her bare behind.
Dog sees her sigh, her hands
tremble, the tears form
in the corners of her eyes.

She wipes them before they fall
and smiles in Dog's wistful direction.
Purpose, she says, is at best elusive
and probably delusion. . . but
there is a melancholy beauty

to our tragic flesh,
in the flash and sizzle
of our cells decaying in the dark
and shoreless sea of time
where we bob and tread in a moment

so short it is measureless. As I
lay next to you just now,
breathing, any overspill of my last
customer mixing with yours and dying
in the chemical sea inside me,

I felt miraculous, but also sad:
a vessel, but also a murderess. She
looks away, toward the dirty window
where daylight forms a bleak puddle.

A customer told me his dream:
that the world *is* a dream, but
also a Zen garden: rocks

and earth and trees placed just so,
light sailing pure through space. . .
but, he told me, to know it is so
does not make it so, and I
was confused. Blood

runs down the hills, he said,
and planes bruise the sky

with metal and noise,
and the words in our mouths
are not pebbles or raindrops

but bullets and arrows,
and then he cried and would not stop.
I left him there, not knowing
what else to do. Camille tucks
her blouse into her leather skirt.

Dog covers his bandages with ragged
clothes and walks her to the street. A cab
honks like bird song made of steel.
A mother screams at her son like a crow
scoffing. Distant gunshots fall as thunder

over the buildings. Dog
jumps involuntarily and Camille holds
him on the top step, kisses him
long, until he is breathless and shaking.
She whispers: there are no trees

in this Garden of Eden, only
marks on our foreheads to measure
the future, to map its sullen terrain,
and the gun-metal blue cost of our complicity
is how all our stories have become meaningless, noise.

Our forlorn tales now add up, endlessly,
to ignorance and loss, compounding
interest on a debt. We no longer
dream and have forgotten how to sing.
This is the litany of our days, Dog,

but our tragedy is less that they end
than that they flow one into another
without reliable witness. You say
you want to be the wind that rises
from the wine-dark sea of praise,

but how would you talk on against
time, and to sing what?

☐

A deadly El Dorado rolls
slowly by. The riders
in wrap-around sunglasses
pass a bottle from hand
to hand, blood of their own blood,

invisible bites of their own flesh
in their teeth. Dog clenches
his good fist, feels pain shoot
up his arm and through his chest,
wishes them death

under his breath. Would you
destroy them all, asks Camille?
or just beat them into civility?
starve them? throw them in prison?
take their loved ones

so nothing remains? They
been there already, Dog, choked
on too much of nothing. Nothing
is what leads here, to bare
knuckle, 44 magnum despair. . . .

So I am to smile, asks Dog,
and thank them for the lead still
in my body, for entrance and exit
scars, for fear? Apologies
are for the innocent, says Camille,

and ain't none of us that.
The El Dorado begins to beat
like a drum, like God's heartbeat,
as it turns the corner.

Camille squeezes Dog
between his legs and giggles
like a girl, skips down
the steps, and walks toward
downtown, hips sliding

back and forth in the exaggerated
walk of her profession, a Pavlovian
sign in search of a response. She
watches herself pass in the reflection
of a store's window, Dog is certain,
to make sure she is still here.

Back in his room, Dog
naps. . . and dreams God
stares from a fence post

into the moon-red eyes
of rabbits. They can't see
Him, but sense His presence

in the direction of the sun.
One will die to feed His divine
form, its blood mix with His.

In dream Dog wonders how
God can take this responsibility
so lightly.

Dog removes his bandages,
packs his few clothes
into a knapsack, and walks
to the road. He
will head inland, alone,
in Walt Whitman's big shoes.
He will chart America

as wilderness. He
will look for home. . . .

Dog's Confession

The stone knows the boundary
of its mineral skin by water's
rush and swirl. The tree
knows the limits of its reach
by wind escaping through out-
stretched arms. Dog knows he
is alive because he aches.

He waits for the sun on the mission
steps shivering, his withered arm
and his wounds sending sheets
of quaking lightning to his brain.
He starts at a grizzled man
in rags who steps from shadow
and throws his aubade at the east
like a fist, as he resolves
the momentary world to simple,

epic truth: today, sunrise
will be a hole in the sky, a rotten
mongrel carcass beside the highway
under the last angry morsel
of the moon, a train whistle
shot from the distance
like a coyote's grief and hung
on the air like Christ.

The man crosses himself as the priest
swings the big doors wide and, wielding
his crucifix like an ax, cutting
the cloud of his breath, blesses
the stairs, Dog and the old man,
the piss-stained curb, the whole
cold world beyond his sanctuary,
his tiny island of light.

Men, cradled in their own arms,
appear out of the crepuscular dark

from all directions and march
like prisoners up the steps. Their eyes
dart, furtive, from behind some barrier
as the eyes of an animal from a burrow.
Dog knows that look: fear-become-compulsion.

These men are the hunted-
by-everything. Seen and unseen
predators lurk everywhere
beyond the gates of their vision,
and for some even in the black cave
behind their eyes: all hunters
the One Hunter, omnivorous
and hungry and pandemic as air.

Such a man will die of fright:
in the alley behind a liquor store,
before his TV, at his desk,
in a strip joint, on a mountain
like a tombstone, on faded
kitchen linoleum, at the sink,
at the lathe, at night
or in full sun, in the braided
embrace of nothing, in the awkward
silence of a realization without words
to equal it. . . alone.

The priest too. Dog
sees fear in his eyes, but also
the hint of madness which Dog knows
is transubstantiated compassion, love
and belief turned to decaying stone
in the face of unending, growing, suffering.
The priest's knuckles are white
as he clutches the cross.

Bless you, he says in monotone
as Dog limps into the glare
of the church, as the doors slam
shut behind him with a mediaeval
creak and bang.

In the church basement
there is only the clank of spoons
against the backdrop of an abysmal
silence. Gruel and toast. Coffee.

The priest must pray before they eat.
Dear God, grown men brood,
he says, whether natural law
or something we learn by osmosis

from our fathers, no one can say. . .
but of course only a woman cries,
but that is a cliché, or maybe a truism.
Who can tell from so close a vantage. . . ?

He goes on for ten minutes,
the gruel steaming, coffee
going cold, the men quiet as graven
images, their unkempt heads bowed.

Dog strains to hear the snap
and sizzle of them trying to make sense
of what they are hearing, but these men
are beyond the attempt.

The priest's words dissipate
with the steam. Our Father,
he says, who art. . . and stops
abruptly. Eat, he says, and sits.

No redemptive revelation, no talk
of sacrifice to yield purification,
recompense, regeneration after
the long and nightmare infested
sleep of these men's souls.

Theology of crisis gives way
to stasis, to walking sleep, walking
death. Dog longs to hear the howl
of these angels who fell, demonic
screams as they are broken in pieces,
trampled; he longs to see deep horror
in their eyes if nothing else.

Then, with the nonchalance of the dead,
the aubade singer falls face first
into his gruel. Dog lifts the man's head
by his unwashed hair, and lays him
gently on the floor as the rest eat on.
He answers their appalling silence:

Some archaeologist of the future
will find runes, tales of pestilence,
a curse on this man's scapula, incised
there by the teeth of the universe
as it devoured him. . . will read there
the text of his suffering.

There will be no script of your passage. . .
our passage. . . left to decipher. Our husks,
brittle exoskeletons filled with nothing
but stifling air, will rot to dirt in the blink
of an eye without a single tooth mark. I
would damn you, but you have damned yourselves.

Dog picks up the aubade singer, a perverse
pieta, the dead heraldic son in the arms
of the suffering son, and carries him outside.
He lays the ragged body on the cold steps,
raises his arms to the east where the rising sun
is caught between buildings.

He sings: May this man descend into primordial
dew, may he descend with tenderness into the involute
music of earth, may he achieve the thunderous
silence of absolute clarity. . . May the pale parchment

of his skin, his voice that was the breath of the horse
of being, awaken me, finally.

Death plays the trombone
in the somber jazz band
of Dog's imagination,

plays sweet and deep
until Dog sleeps like a child
beside the cold, blue highway

that will lead to the land
of his progenitors, the reservation
where his grandmother died

on the High Plains
of America, halfway
between sea and shining sea. . .

but Dog dreams:

he walks west from the road,
past stone stelae, over
fields of weeds at the margins

of forests, walks for forty days
in a straight line, sleeps
forty nights in the wilderness
of the imagination.

There is nothing human here
except what Dog carries with him:
the heavy bag of memory,
the bright knife of desire. . .
and these he knows will dim
eventually, grow lighter, duller. . .
and then what? The silence of animals?

Their inconspicuous velocity? Their
defiant awareness? The unrelentingly
beautiful monotone of the earth without us?

Dog wakes in a cold sweat under the last
fragment of the moon. He throws
his voice at the sky, an exultant tremolo
of grief. He howls. He walks, west. . . .

The Book of Allegory

Poem for the Magician of the Dance

. . .love and the imagination
are of a piece,
swift as the light
to avoid destruction. . . .

NOT prostrate, to copy nature,

but a dance

William Carlos Williams

The witch doctor in love with language
as the arrow of imagination — the word
as amorphous brick to build shifting dance halls,
syllables as seed for the flowers of truth —
demands to sleep the restless slumber
of longing within you, to fill you
slowly with want like the masculine
organ in its feminine sheath until
you reciprocate with a fire to equal his
and dance, together, reader with absent speaker,
on the undulating ground of the poem,
in the dazzling vortex of the human capacity
to make and remake.

This is, after all, the dance of being: slight
in form, fragile and frenetic as love,
the brave and mutant blossom of interpretation
passes through finite lips and teeth, up from the bowels
and unattainable heart, to vibrate as spore
on the fine and fretful air of the mind.

It is true, the race stumbles unconsciously
toward singularity, the fusion to end time; but
the weaver-of-spells utters from behind the veil
to remind us: subject and object remain
forever separate where they circle one another
on the field of the page — the complete universe

of people and things — as lovers, whose urgency
to embrace, to become if even for a moment

the same vibrating substance, is all that turns
us toward one more day, a redemptive hunger
that ceases only with our last breath.

Poetry in an Age of Empire

An anonymous line on the wind.
Halting iambs of death across the sky.
Reluctant bellowing like an explosion:

a young man tied to a tree
implores the sons of peasants
in sweat-stiff uniforms to listen,
to understand his words as men:

despair is a constellation
of flame at the base of the skull.
desire an oceanic blossom
in our blood. . . .

We, you and I, are nothing
but erections and tears,
the manic oscillation between.
Our songs are made of this.

His guards, numb, but not yet
with regret, stare at blood-red clay
on their boots, pull smoke
from cigarettes with the stunted

dignity of the damned
breathing the first acrid air of hell,
and pretend not to hear.

Poem for Gerald, Who Gave up Poetry for Booze

It is the precarious joy of living
that rolls from your ornately
enameled tongue as you beseech
me to breathe one time for you,
your own breathing a cracked
and fluid mirror but tarnished
like wet copper where it stumbles
over the open esophageal wound
of your dis-ease.

You whispered to me once,
hoarse with song and smoke,
drunk on mescal: the poet
is obliged to blaspheme. . .
and another time, an oblique
echo of Rilke: praise is all
language does.

Now the shadow of Death
whispers to you from its perch
on your left shoulder, and you
talk back, your voice thin as blood.
I have heard you in sleep
these last cold days telling
Death of the God in stones
and birds, the grief in man,
and the desperation of all
to be song.

Soon enough it will be my turn
to speak or fall into abysmal silence.
If nothing else I hope to say
I knew an old man who loved
humanity and earth enough to curse
both, whose failure to utter
ate him from the inside out.

Gerald's Song (Homocentrism Breeds Apocalypse)

He died of the famine
of spirit, an antimonast
drunk among the blank
sunflower faces of the masses
who turn to follow what
they are told to follow. He
groveled before men with money,
before women who promised
golden snatch and breasts
like coursing horses.
He did not care whether I breathed
prayer or poison. The day
his heart stopped he told me
a man is measured by his line
of credit, how much ass
he's had, his hunger for more
of everything.

The day his heart stopped
I sent my last message,
although I have drained
many bottles since that would
hold them on the waters of time:
The language of man
has become the language
of Death. Love equals
an old man's wrinkled arms
on a sheet, his splintered breath
that never shaped air to say
owl, vetch, cobweb, dream. . .
never said dance, being,
blessed are. . . never said
son.

Gerald in Darkness

Every time I see the Pleiades
holding hands in their eternal
game of ring-around-the-roses
I am reminded I am small.

Once, I begged those sisters-
sans-mercy to plead my case with God,
who is, as it turns out, a purblind
dotard behind the fatal veil

of the dark. They refused.
So now I hide under the sinister
umbrella of street lamps, look
at my feet as I walk from one

sightless circle of light to the next,
and pretend not to notice
the unbearably tiny sound
of my steps in snow.

Requiem

I rock in the arms of grief,
in dream, where you are road kill,
the last piece of your lung
finally heaved up, a sword
of broken white lines stained
with whiskey and blood run
through your belly.

The crow of desire eats
your eyes, grows
sad on your vision,
and squawks a last message
another voice you borrowed
as you borrowed mine
at me:

       Read well
the script of the skin,
the language of gravity
and remorse no less
than love, this singing
in the cells that is blazing
neon curving toward nothing,

electrical impulse tapping
constant noise at the sky,
at other skin bundles
also tapping. . . . Then
crow flies away, your spirit
stone-heavy in his gut.

I fell down in the road
under the thumb of nothing,
once. Cringed, cried,
lacking courage to stand or die.

I squat next to you
to tell your corpse this,
that I dared not speak
when awake, to you alive. . .

how after the sky lifted
I limped home, hid
for days in the dark.
How your end is my end.

Father I met in a drunken
alley, it is the seed
of nothing left in me I fear,
but also the you in me

staring out at the world
covered in dark chitin, word-
less, smoldering, churning
with Spartan breath that refuses to form.

Sun rises through mist
that rises from the west
to meet the light head-
to-head at my window.

It has been two years
since I saw you walk the highway
toward home, a non-specific place,
east. I know the earth

has swallowed you, taken
you to its bosom, caressed
you to dust. All you ever
wanted. What you feared most.

Today, I will visit the street
where black birds sing raucous
chorus to passing cars, to me. I
will resist the urge

to cry or pray or sing
my own dirge under leafless
cottonwoods. I will say
to the overbearing sky,

I knew an old man
who loved humanity and earth
enough to curse both, whose
failure to utter ate him.

Enlightenment

> *Ain't no way around it,*
> *no matter how hard you try,*
> *life is hard then you die. . . .*
> Traditional Blues

He is the Buddha of indiscretion, blues man
with a fretted tongue, the one makes you hunger
for your sister, go to work on sweet wine and pills,
hand rummaging in the till, the one who turns
you inside out with jealousy and desire, shoots
the dog for dreaming, accepts the neighbor's wife's
tart kisses. He is that tattered one who bleeds
before the mirror, demanding salvation, screaming
for sleep, who finally says, *enough,* and walks
from that day forward with the wind and stars
for company, with the devout and ecstatic heartache
of a breathing man.

Queen's Song

All saints in America are of commerce
and addiction now, in this dark spot of prayer
we call our lives, in this dream become compulsive
apparition at the edge of vision, shuddering
off to die in some crumbling, dust-ridden corner
like an unwanted old woman. . .

like Anne-of-a-Thousand-Sorrows who sleeps
on the radiant metal grate in the post office foyer,
who talks to patrons from her untoward dreams
as they pass into the great postal dark without looking at her,
as they return to the light, to radios ringing, to cellular
phones folded like a tomb in electronic slumber.

I stumble, she says in my imagination, *under
the sagging baggage that is my flesh, under scars
so long they trail behind me in the wind,
so thick and granite-hard that if I had a bed
I would still sleep on stone, on steel,
so repulsive ten thousand layers of rags
will not hide them.*

*But under these creases and canyon-
like folds is the face of Nefertiti: high
cheekboned and almond-eyed, casting
hungry images on the rain, weaving
the deep mythology of survival
into this misshapen bulk for all to see. . .*

*and under these clothes, beneath this skin
wrapped as in burial rags for the journey
to the other side, my queen's body dances
imperceptibly, full fledged and whole in her sex,
tits small and firm, ass thin as a raven's cough.*

*This is my song: hiding in hag-form, sign
and symbol for an age, is a goddess
made of what we could have been; and woven*

into a crone's breath is the singing
of an angel whose spells are of the now twin
gods, beauty and murder, sacrificial
roses I would push like knives through the heart
of all human shame.

Father Hunger

Your father walks in the sun, his
hands in his pockets, his eyes
transfixed on the ground
as if the earth were treacherous.

You tell him you need to hear
his voice. He mumbles
that he is short of money
for a new car. You

tell him that you love
him. He says he is lonely,
that his shoes were too tight
when he was a child,

that blood soaked his socks
as he walked by the bully's
house on his way to school
under dead trees. You tell

him about the opium tea
you drank alone in the mountains
at seventeen, how you saw
his thoughts across the miles

as breasts hung from trees,
the nipples small bursts
of light like stars beckoning
just out of reach of his lips.

He says he is hungry, the day
frightfully warm. He says
his father was a silent man.
He says. . . .

The Message

And pluck till time and times are done
The silver apples of the moon,
The golden apples of the sun.
                    Yeats

The solid leaf wall
of this tree is towering
injunction to a man
without nerves, mute,
violently silent except
for the tiny electric sound
of his skin twitching
in the shadows where fallen
fruit stinks like overwrought
wine. . . but this too
                    is a message
from the earth
even he can understand.

Love, the tree speaks
with its involute tongues,
can grow sad as metaphor,
turn, fall forever toward
the humus that begat it,
recede until all but madness
is equivocal, until
a man must turn inward
like the multifold whorls
of this cambial heart,
                    or die.

The man looks upward
at the impenetrable exchange
of shadow and light
and tries to imagine a soul,
mysterious and inflammable,
at center, maybe, already aflame.

For the Woman Who Would Have Me
Guess the Color of Her Panties

I dream of eating
the midnight blue snack
of you. Tender, creamy
bites, tart. . . delicious
and dangerous like a prisoner's
                        last meal. . .

or maybe this treat
is saffron, lightning bolt
of pineal delight to savage
                the synapse. . .

or blazing orange chiffon,
the color of sunset to melt
in my mouth like sugared snow. . .

or perhaps smashed fingertip
mauve overlaid with neon
chartreuse, a synesthetic
taste bud orgasm. . .

or maybe scarlet, intense
blood-color of the pulse
in the head, of vehement want. . .

or, sadly, maybe the color
is frigid pink, the tongue
frozen to winter steel. . .

or worse, black. . . the universe
crushed to a lightless ball,
to the nothingness of a ribald
philosopher's nightmare.

I will choose that first dream:
the midnight blue wonder of you

as excitable feast, savored
for a long moment, regardless

of what else comes: sated sleep
or the long decay of starvation
after tasting what only a god
has the strength to touch once
                  and never again behold.

Empathy

He stood motionless inside her,
weightless, invisible, a spark
at the center of her being. He
felt the aureoles of her nipples
warm and stiffen, the soft spot
she touched with her finger
flush and go moist. He felt
her breath twist into the syllables
of his own name as it passed
through her teeth and over her lips
into unbridled air. He felt this across
many miles and heard, just barely,
fear flow into the music of his name
as it rolled out of the glacial dark
where she stored everything she wished
did not exist, the mouth of a beast
he could not, dared not, touch.

Remembering a Photo of Breasts

A Pre-Rafaelite Nude Study, Anonymous
Circa 1920

They must be holy, these lidless
eyes that stare into the soul of a man,
because I shiver from heart to genitals
the sacred shimmy of desire-become-
devotion at the mere memory of those hills
of earthen stuff cast in silver to escape
time, the fonts at which children, men,
many hungry others, must have sighed;
even if, now, they are shrunken nets full
of heavy metal or, more likely, actual
earth, the last tender quiver into the final
dissolve some loved one's fading memory.

I would sing hosanna except for my lover's
tit in my mouth, a sweet bite of living planet.
I would sing for those ancient but forever
nubile breasts on a lost page, for the breast
my sons' mother fed them from,
for the breast my mother never gave to me
but that nourished me nonetheless,
for this breast that sustains me now,
although no milk flows from it. . . .

The fleeting jiggle and flash on a screen
to sell beer or cars robs us daily
of the sacred taste of flesh; but, once,
a photographer's lamp bathed some hard-
luck flapper, eternal mother, forever
lover, in light like the moon's.

The End of Language

My tongue moves
over your breasts,
a bee-child sashaying
through flowers.

Maybe, this is the flash-
point of language, the place
act consumes symbol,
the ground where the snake
of the sign devours the tail
of its own significance.

How else to say song-
of-flesh, tender beast,
salt and sugar on my fingers
and on my breath

than to show you?

Parable

The great Caravaggio
was commissioned to make
an angel. He painted
a single bird's wing
emerging from dark canvas,
stained it with molten silver,
feather tips blazing.

The rich man stared
at the shadow where wing
became darkness, disappeared
to void, could not pry his eyes
from the wing-pit, from space
where light should spill
like money.

Furious, he refused to pay
for what he could not see
and made Caravaggio famous.
To this day stupid men
chop wings from living birds,
dip them in melted coin,
call their work divine.

The Herbalist

She walks in the spirit land
of yellow banner, purple gentian,
ghostly bistort, three
shades of blue phlox, infinite
green, an anonymous red
darker than Grandmother's
blood bitters. . .

       a land where breath
itself rises from earth
as sexual electricity
to hold in the hand,
where light is tied into vortical
knots to caress her cheek,
the residue of light flowing down
her soft nasal tissue, esophageal
tunnel, lung temple.

Blue bolts of pineal delight
shudder her. She remembers.
The old woman led her
to a field of blue flax
on her seventh birthday, told
her to dance for her beauty,
to drink the blossoms
for protection from sorcery,
to heat and moisten pains
in the breast. Grandmother
drank this tincture herself
against coming cold and pleurisy,
but mostly to dull old aches
she did not explain.

She took to gentian bitters
her last year of life, a fresh
batch fermented and distilled daily

in season, excess stored for winter.
To lift chronic exhaustion of old age,
says the book. To comfort the heart,
said the old woman, and to ease
the pain of cold or evil lodging
that accumulates over years

                              in the chest.

Now, her grandmother dead since fall,
she understands. Sepal
and stamen blow kisses over
radiant ground to no one. Fierce
and resplendent syllables that pass
through the lips of flowers,
into and back out of her, are God's
true name; but no one touches *her* lips,
no one has ever whispered her name.

In a Year of Drought. . .

thunderheads move over the land
as a raging father, all impotent
bluster. No water touches earth,
but evaporates halfway here: love
held out and pulled away
in the same motion by someone
who cannot cry.

Or, storms fly over our heads
without stopping, the prodigal
in black coat, light screaming
from his sleeves, his flaming
voice a distant reminder of old
wounds only constant flight
                         can heal.

Or, storms simply do not come.
Today absence rides a hot wind,
smells of mortal dust and eternal
milk, a mother without whose touch
no child lives.

The old man mourns as prairie cracks
under the yellow thumb of the sun.
Tonight he will lift his arms
to the great lung of the sky
as a full moon rises, sun still
bloody on the hills, to pull
down thunder. Ozone crisp
and horse shit smell will mix,
linger, groundsel and sage strain
toward the few drops that fall. One here.
One there.

Then the clouds will pass,
and the old man, and the plants
that are his charges, will bow
their heads to the hot earth,

to stilted dreams that augur
the first stiff brown steps
in the dance of the dead.

Patience: The Heroism of Plants

Octavio Paz

The prairie sighs under the ten-million
tiny fists of the rain. The obverse
of yesterday. Its mirror image.

Yesterday the old man heard earth
scream, a pestilential wail
to break the heart, as the Jews'

hearts were broken in the desert, says he
who was kidnapped to Jesuit school
as a boy, beaten for speaking his father tongue.

He laughs at the geometry of reversal,
chants thanks to the clouds for being,
for conjuring out of the oppressive stillness.

The plants sing with him
of the incandescent power of persistence
that burns, larger than love, in their veins.

Something to Believe In

Locusts hang above the Platte
River from cottonwoods, sing
in their recombinant strength
the song no one will sing again
for seven years, a bug
eternity through which the species
                              sleeps.

This very day they are reborn, shed
their husks to praise, lay eggs
in earth, or fall to water
from on high. Tomorrow
they will swim through trout gut,
                    back to oblivious dirt.

This very day I dream of small
steps through dew-slip and aspen,
of growing quiet with age, dressed
in robes like a monk, each
movement a prayer. This black
that descends on me less scourge
than now, part of the rhythm
                    like breath, like stride.

Want will be pared to air brimful
of sage scent, to lark song,
to voice hammered smooth on a stone
and almost inconspicuous on the wind
as it fades toward the silence of loam,
where what passes for sunspangled
singing among my people is sifted
through time's bloody fingers, torn
atom from tender atom and respun,
more shapely, more pure, one
                    step closer to glory.

The Gravity of Desire

I know nothing but
what makes flesh twitch
and shiver under the waning
March moon shedding pieces
of itself over the confused
earth, a withering blossom
of grief in wind-driven sky.

I long for prayer-like lightning,
loud-spiller-of-buckets.
or the hard sleep winter brings, body
warmed by layers of summer stored
fat. I can stand no more straining
at the threshold of a season,
trying to get in, to get out.

No more descent through
emotion's syrup-thick layers
to the switchblade of silence
that threatens to cut me
ear to ear. No more failed
attempts slicing holes
in the addled night to let in,
or out, the light of the word.

This nether-season spews particles
of fear and want beyond number.
The roan in the field behind my house
knows better than I. When the wind
shifts and pressure drops out
the bottom of the glass, he stands
on his hind legs, beats
the air like a man and screams
at the half gone moon for the absence
of mare, her blown scent blinding him

from a mile. He cannot help himself. March
on the high plains is a dream pulling

as weight at the heart and loins until
the brain contracts into a tight fist of desire
                                 and hammers back.

Poem for a Dead Grizzly

Is this the final renunciation
of our souls? A being beyond
our understanding, like God,
lies naked under Douglas fir,
stripped of her pelt, her power,
her bones green and turning
to earth, weeds sprouting
through vacant sockets,
a blasphemous hole in her temple.

What man did this? What men
exploded the heart of divinity
with 7 magnum millimeters
of blind lead, pissed cheap beer
in roadside bushes by the light
of lightning-bright, bear-blinding
spots mounted on the pickup truck,
then drove away, oblivious.

I read of clean bones in the news,
see killers in my imagination
and shudder, a hot pain in my belly
that has no name. Grief, loss,
vacuum, slice-of-our-collective-
spirit rotten are not enough.
Is this the last day a goddess
awakens from nine months sleep,
wades through showy daisy
and ghost-white bistort, sits
on her fat haunches to moan of love?
The last day praise rises
from the darkest cave as the person
Bear? I must not believe it. Dare not.

Somewhere, seven year locusts sing
a dirge in aspen, final rite
for Brown-Mother-Trundler-through-Trees,
Thunder-on-Four-Paws, Claws-

like-Knives. The locusts remind us
what the slayers, those I cannot forgive
hubris warped unto killing-only-to-kill,
have forgotten: God is eater and eaten,
as are we. It is this and her spirit
smoldering in the black cave of imagination
our ever smaller souls fear, her teeth
like razors, and her resurrection more real,
almost, than we can dream.

Buffalo

For Walt Whitman
Divine am I inside and out. . . .

I want to knit my heart
to the shaggy heart of the beast,
stand sideways to the tempest
of being like God wrapped
in the arms of wind, turn
my fierce eye on America, paw
the ground to make her shiver
to her humanist center, her
melting Christian soul.

                    I want to lay
my savage tongue on the air
with news of what grass knows,
that seeds are arrows on the breeze,
that roots split stones. . . rumble
over earth on sparking hooves
in a wave of untamed creatures
who defy America's fear
of her animal body, our
                    ungulate desire.

I want to charge headlong
protected by spirits, bulletproof
and unafraid, as she shoots narcotic
slugs that do not kill but wound
the spirit so deep death is barely noticed
where he stands over us, his whispers
unheard. Dying no crossing, but mere
hand-tap to signal a more profound sleep.

I want to run in hulking animal form
like a thrown blade from sea
to shining sea, gore holes in the stone-
blindness of men that holds them like a dungeon,

drive them from their dreamless sleep
to streets that will return to prairie, forest,
immaculate dirt under pounding hooves.
I want to push them, relentlessly,
toward air and light and the future
that will rush in their blood like storm.

Optimism Blues

The Specific Gravity of Death

for Sharon

That I love the tangent of your
bottom, where your thigh curves
to the base of your spine like a magical
snake, is undeniable. . . that all
signs in the human universe
add up to the specific gravity
of death is more problematic.

You see, I am looking
for that supreme fiction, clarity. . .
for some truth in the random world
that won't let us down, a singular
assertion to stand the test of lived
reality, a consanguine *beauty* or *faith*
or *wisdom* spoken in the wing beats
of birds, some more than dime-store
daemon awakened in humankind
that speaks back, suddenly disdainful
of our current violations. I want us
to be, once again, ecstatically alive
in our heavily discounted Eden.

You stand before me, oblivious
to the infinite herd of my sorrows
big as two-humped camels, your
unbearable nakedness sparking
like St. Eve's, brazen as starlight
on the sea, a momentary dream,
an elemental correspondence
with everything. . . and I shudder
in my exile, surprised
by the urge to pray.

The Allegory of an Academic Tuesday

The hound's voice rises
along a counterfeit wave-
length of discovery. A frozen
body hides somewhere among
rock and carrion fowl, but not here.

Here the wanton professor's
shoes engross him like a woman's
tender breasts as the books
under his arm twist and slither
imperceptibly, beyond him

in the dither the world mistakes
for certainty. The ghost of Derrida
bows in the trees to ravens
that mock his insouciant presence.
Not even a dry bone to eat, they say,

before flapping away like burial
boats on the air. The professor
turns the corner at the end
of a hopeless boulevard
where vagrant children of rich
men laugh like uppity orangutans,

children whose mothers have abandoned
any notion their wombs are miraculous,
their tears meaningful. The hound
of desire strays into the dead air space
between stars, between Volvos at the curb,

lays his head full of quandary
on his big front paws and sleeps,
even the violence of dream
but a playful whisper
he no longer understands.

Aphasiac in Paradise

To locate yourself in the omnivalent sign,
some voluminous heaven that haunts
the mind of every man and woman
who has walked the travail of living:
a blue and pale flower luminous
on the wind even as it is tossed
like a kitten from the jaws of a bear,
upward and out, forever rising. . . but no,
now down into the open maw of a god
hell-bent to devour it all.

We dream this time outside
of time, where our lover's nipples
harden forever under the wisp
of our breathing, where
the tongue effloresces silence
into the priceless name of our nightmare
deity, where praise is the answer
to everything.

I know the word for death-
beyond-blindness. I know
the word for singing-to-equal-life.
I know the word for love-that-is-not-
an-illusion. But my mouth
will not open, and there is no cipher,
no hand signal, no sign
to render this despair.

Dream of a Dead Poet

For Gerald

He holds his self-murdering hand over
the elegant earth and raises his licked
thumb to the west, divining what wind
shed his blood that seeps through the duff,
a dozen years of pine needle rot.

He says, *the viscous fingers*
of the dead tremble as they spread
into the soil, as they splay into a thinner
and thinner grasp and finally disappear
into the melt that is the elemental
puddle, the absolute dissolve.

Then he flutters away, distracted
by all the movement around him,
his message hanging on the air
like smoke. Poets in the omnivorous
silence, we are strangers here:

our words beautiful as bird song,
but, to our great sadness,
as insubstantial. The light
declines down the western world
and all I have to say floats off
toward the clouds that stride,
like inattentive gods, over the edge
of the known universe.

A Dirge for Things

Isn't the secret intent
of this taciturn earth, when it forces lovers together,
that inside their boundless emotion all things may shudder with joy?

. . .

Speak and bear witness. More than ever
the Things that we might experience are vanishing, for
what crowds them out and replaces them is an imageless act.

Rilke

Even awake we cannot stop dreaming, and all
our dreams are of a glowering absence our indifferent
fingers absently fold, over and over, from memory,
some vestigial urge that holds us like a vision
we barely remember: when the thing in our fist
could save our lives, our souls, could break our hearts
for the piece of the maker *it* held like a hand holds
a hand. . . arrow, pot, poem, portrait of a lady
mourning, tender cakes, a photo of breasts.

I am calm now before this reckoning
that never comes, that does not flower
perversely with cost, its sinister odor
beckoning us out of this waking sleep
and toward death. . . where we have filed
our tools, baskets, striped serapes, fish hooks,
bone-handled knives, earthen baking ware,
silver hair clips, our own faces painted
black and garish red like ghosts.

I am calm now in our forgetting
that the subtle breath of matter was inflamed
by a far reaching human psyche whose closure
must certainly portend a demonic boredom,
a wretched loneliness, an earth
                    that can do without us.

The Limits of Empathy in a Dark Age

It is the eternal picture of spilled
blood, of laughter floating over a man
caught transforming into a corpse,
the insistent spectacle of the death
card as it emerges out of thin air
in a nondescript field where flowers
flame to stars, the legerdemain
for which our species is famous.

The knife glitters with pleasure,
bullets sigh in their nests
and we, the lookers-on, stare
into the wilderness of the human
mind, know tangentially both power
and its absence, feel momentarily
our equally famous grief. . .

then, we turn the page, as if the entire
world were awash in sunlight,
as if our shadows could swallow
memory, transmogrify it into charity.
How else do we live without our heads
bowed? How else sleep without screaming?
How kiss our children's foreheads,
that are perfect blossoms straining
toward the sky, as if winter
                              would never come?

Song for the Dead

> *I would not have thought*
> *Death had undone so many. . . .*
> Dante

People from television map
what the dead call their lives, sing
in their moldy dreams of times
that never existed, wealth,
a purgatorial bliss, beauty
to make the genitals quiver
like a loosed bow string, to make
the strong weep in this land both
mythically pristine and so powerful
to the taste buds the dead are satisfied
and famished at the same time.

The dead walk sideways under
the fleeting sun, breathe, wave
for a cab. The dead sparkle
in their own blunted imaginations.
The dead sigh and swear off
cigarettes. The dead talk of love
and deli meat and ice storms,
of vulgar automobiles from Taipei
and aching shoes and bleating
prostitutes and organic rice
and turnovers-to-die-for.

The dead in their dream.
The dead in our way.
The dead who are sad
without knowing it, whose
teeth chatter in the vaguely
sacred night. . . as close
to the engine of creation
as they dare stand.

Portents

I count the birds of ill
omen like overdue bills,
as a signal of failure
on a cosmic scale, gore
stain fresh on their beaks,
death fragrant in the long
primary feathers on which
they wheel against a virgin
sky. I swear I can smell
them from here: the stale
black of my sorrows
that mount the wind like a god
turned inside out with want,
that spin a kinetic and olfactory
mantra over this highway,
this 90 mph, this savage thirst
to say something that matters
without stuttering. . . a psalm
of loss to devour the world.

Optimism Blues

And so many of the universe forget themselves
Who are the great forgetters
Who will know just how to make us forget such and
such a part of the world.
       Guillaume Apollinaire

In the brisk and bluest corners
of my imagination, the wild
heart survives yet in these creatures
who bask in their tameness like old cats
in late sun as it drains through suburban
windows, imperturbable in their comfort,
sleeping.

In the corners of my imagination
where the west wind molests
the greening earth to shuddering
orgasm, the sleepers can still rise,
dance like leaves over the vortical
ground, whisper erotic messages
above the static that humps the air-
ways, can laugh in their somnambulists' dreams.

In the brightest corner where the sun
has been sentenced but hangs on tenuously
to godhead, where breath equals praise
and all praise settles in the sun's breast
pocket like a fancy kerchief, the human
heart has not forgotten it's animal rhythm,
its corporeal *thrum. . . thrum. . . thrum. . .*
beautiful beyond all reckoning, sad
beyond all telling, glorious like singing
in the mouth of the eternal and valiant
sun as it strides toward deicide.

Insomnia

The great pale horse of the wind
vies for supremacy with the blue
horse of the mind, stallions standing
on their hind legs, blood-sharp
front hooves flashing under
the thinnest of moons. . . as the mad
cheer for the diaphanous, big-shouldered
one in his rage, because he owns the earth
tonight and will not take no for an answer.

The mad in death's pancake makeup,
insolence stains in their teeth, yellow
eyes glowing faintly. The mad
who are effluvia, rejectamenta, white
noise, ten thousand confused plans
for escape, ten thousand succinct
excuses for failure, sad detritus
of all wooden declarations, unnamed
hungers growing bolder, the devil's
brides whose tongues of ancient
crumbling steel flick between my lips
and down my throat.

The ghost horse of the wind now bites
the horse of the mind as if to devour him,
and the mad grow inevitably louder,
their applause anti-rhythmic, a sudden
burst of thousand-branched thunder
to which I surrender. I pray to that blustering
clamor in the dark, beg it for silence,
and name it finally my *self* under
the oppressive sky that is the ceiling,
from my bed that is a storm-tossed boat
moving, slow as death, toward morning.

Memory

The way this leaps,
the mind about its tangential
business, from smarmy
to profound in a nanosecond:

what was it we said in the dark
while waiting for our lives to combust
into something miraculous, beyond
words? . . .the sighing and raw scraping

of human voice in ecstatic warning
that this *is* a miracle, the only one
we are allowed: sweat and jism
and the vast vocabulary of desire

boiled to simple syllables, to mnemonics
that bring you back now, naked
on the edge of the bed, of my life,
smiling as if from beyond the grave.

For an Ex-Wife

Recall me in chains
meat after roses soar
sadly out from love

      Read me repulsive
      robed in lies produced
      of urges and sordid visions

Send me mercy over
the airwaves and I will configure
our story out of earth and stone

      an unfinishable monument,
      the rooms filled forever
      with a negligent half light,

with syllables as empty
as your hand, and your shadow
eternally dissolving.

Love Poem

A jaguar flames in my blood, beats
its beautiful head against the cluttered
walls of my veins, pacing. . . pacing,
tearing at the seams that separate
my days, growling the samba
if I try to sleep.

                    But when
the big cat rolls over in his own
restless dream my heart grows teeth,
a feline sensitivity to darkness, and I
am nothing but fleetness, an angular
density of muscle and fluted bone.

You smile, and I want to lick
the length of you, to kill something
large and brooding, to lay it
at the altar of your feet.

Snapshots of Dreamland

This is the dream where trees
are carnivorous and the sky
lowers an angry head to push
me to the ground. There is never
more. I wake up here, always,
swimming in the black sea
of a room that is not the blacker
sea of the grave, but worse,
the stench of life more over-
whelming than death.

This is the dream where the gravity
of some final surmise mounts me
like a perverse dog to shove
me from behind through a portal
the shape of my own face, outward
toward the place where atoms
refuse to ever reconvene.

This is the dream where you
lower your breasts to my mouth,
first the left, then the right. Where
I imagine you, in the dream,
as big as a house I long to enter,
but I can never image
a key to fit your precious lock
and, here too, awake sweating.

And this dream ends all dreaming:
the map to another world
is in my fist, an X to mark
the spot where this world will shudder
to a stop. Notice the unnatural gleam
in my eye, a poet's brazenness
to imagine such a place. Here,
I do not know whether to weep

or throw a party for all ghosts
in a desperate act of kinship.

They will certainly rise to meet me,
if only to drink cheap scotch and bottles
of Bohemia, for in the invitation
can be read the bleak stretches
of mind where I am the tether
between the dark and the light, what
this dream itself whispers. Think
of it, my love. This minute the dead
raise their glasses and call me brother,
sharer of their most prized secret.

Dreaming the Salvation of the World

In the low throat of a pale herdsman
a guttural note of joy is stranded.

His eyes will not close for dreaming.
His heart will not open for death.

But the new sheep bawl all afternoon
and into the night, their cries spike-hard.

And every morning his tender eyelids
ache with the possibility of lions, wolves,

thieves. His is a hero's strength,
dazzling in its implication

for the larger world. But then
the secret voices begin to rise

from the grass, from the watering hole,
from the hair on his dog's back,

saying, *tomorrow is a coin you have
been robbed of. . .* saying,

*your blood will spill as a martyr's.
Holy the blood. Holy the day*

*the sheep wander over the edge
of the earth, holy the sleep*

*of the man whose dream
is the salvation of the world.*

His eyes close to the music
of lambs bleating,

the dream already real.

Allegory of the Broken Blood Vessel

For Alyson

Her iris, hovering like the moon
over the blood spot where it strives
to blot out the absolute white
of the eye's heaven, searches
each face for a sign, some hint
a single word exists to equal
the involute reticulations of eternity,
to light us all ablaze with visions,
to turn our mouths to cauldrons
of possibility chanting *as if*. . .
as if. . . *as if*. . . amid the carnage.

Planting

For Rilke and for Bill Doreski

I want to speak in translation,
to say to the taciturn earth
in tones it understands
that we walk here among
blazing raindrops and sunlight
as ghosts of an older understanding,
ciphers for a truth the universe
cannot know without this fading
remnant of music:

The swallows, larks, and sparrows
are numberless gestures on the sky,
in the darkening hand spreading
over the earth like the passion
that sucks our breath outward
and into the savage waves of the air.
I crumble dirt through my fingers
and walk this ground
         as if for the first time.

Canary in a Mine Shaft

For Christopher

The multiple vertical horizons
he stares through daily remind
him. His knuckles, bleeding,
remind him. The voluptuous
dark seething at the center
of the earth where he lives,
threatening a silence he cannot
defeat, reminds him: his parcel
is hard labor in a hard time.

Seeking guidance, he bangs
with cold chiseled words
on Vallejo's locked door in Paris
where the old poet forever dreams
a highway the shape of a grave,
any way out of this terrifying
responsibility: to speak, to defy
mediocrity, to breathe in a form
that will shudder the world awake.
Where, forever, as if Hell were acceptance
of the world's need, the rain falls
like a premonition and Vallejo
writes himself to death.

Visions of Banality at the Airport

We ride underground in the belly
of a snake, terminal to concourse
in a perverse reversal of death,
and back, a mockery of rebirth.

I can barely breathe, going
or coming. Ions of air
switch polarity under the subtle
onslaught of atmospheric violence

that is so many minds confined
to this stainless steel space. Slate
blue bolts ricochet near the ceiling, and
I smell singed hair and synapses smoldering;
or, perhaps, it is the lack of drama

makes me daydream of dying. So many lives
amiable as milk, all suffering homogenized
to penetrate the entire substance, an appearance
of purity. Heroism strained out with the flies.

A man in gray toupee stares at his shoes. A young
woman with bare arms, a tattoo of St. Michael
on her breast, stares at the conundrum of his shoes
too. Lovers grope into the magnificent
distance between them: a chasm,

an incipient grief, a universe where they project
the dream of a soul melded to a soul. The doors
open blindly, and, my head light, I cannot move
as my fellow passengers slough onto the escalator
to flee this underworld without ghosts or penance.

The inside of the snake is pale and distraught,
air after an echo, an emptiness ten times empty
where once there was at least the combined breathing

of all that potential for vision, however muted,
however sluggish. The doors whisper shut,
and I ride towards death, wishing aloud
to again see the stars, for one more birth.

It is Nearly a Cliché. . .

now that the universe of right angles
and a simple yes or no has dissolved
through permutation, potentiality,
to the black hole of chaos tight as a fist:
a butterfly in China flaps yellow wings

and, ten-thousand leagues away, births
a hurricane. An act of faith so complex
human imagination buckles and all *what if*
congeals, turns cold as death, terrified
silence the popular response.

Even so, I speak and a billion wings
churn, and as many poets' voices,
as many birds singing the trade winds;
even so, a child spinning circles in the park
with arms outstretched turns the air
                              to raging turbulence. . .

and, somewhere, a man and woman reach
for each other, a prisoner is set free, a mind
changed, resolved to provisional clarity
for a split second. All because I speak,
because in China a translucent butterfly,
defying the odds, lifts toward the sun.

Invocation for the New Year

I finally become a man
*   singing among flames. . . .*
                    "Friends on the Road," Neruda

The first day of a new century
and the oracles, who once spoke
from the mouth of quavering flame,
are dead. I walk instead among men
whose strained eyes are the closure
of all frontiers. I limp amid random
sequences of sound falling from the sky
like rain. The corpse of fraternity
will not rise and my stuttering heart
is the tombstone of a thousand voices
from the past that cannot save us.

I want to shout: *this confusion*
is a sin. The darkness of the last
bloody hundred has seeped
into everything, entered the earth
to become the stuff of our soup:
a flowering grain to make
the rankest devil beam.

But the streets will brook
no enigma greater than one
foot placed in front of the other. I
speak under my breath anyway:
to the sun whose fabulous story died
with the prophets, to the moon
whose pimpled face men have trampled,
to the wind whose tongue shatters
all excuses.

I reach for another notebook, a singular
act of desperation to signal a deeper stride

into the perils of manhood. The pages
are blank but dream of words that will spin on
after the libraries have all burned.

Necessary Errata

Flashpoint and Thunder, with Tears

By a trick of light captured and respun
to carry our illusions on its back like a camel,
we are in the opulent city of towers that wave
in the sky as fingers in the face of God,
as accusation and rebuke, that wave in the sky
made small by our lack of imagination, the illusion
of electric-blue cascading over the earth, over
our dissonant dream translated into a thousand
dialects—two-thirds dead in our lifetime—as *dominion*,
as *winner-take-all*, as *devourer-of-whatever-gives-you-identity*.

We are in the opulent city of towers alight
with the fate we have wished upon the maddening poor
costumed in silly rags, our monuments torched, fifty
years of thwarted desire prodded to flame as human
beings fall from the sky like raindrops. Money men,
robed in blood and exclusion, and the innocent alike
watch the ground rise to meet them as the fist
of someone else's fate, arms and legs akimbo
in the 200 mph wind of freefall as they slide
down the knife edge between life and death, a dance
the poor know all too well because this spastic
trembling fills their dreams, their vagrant
wishes they cast at us for want of bombs.

We are in the opulent city of towers and the name
of God is a curse coated in jet fuel. The towers rain
down upon the innocent and the sinners alike, and we
cannot look away for the movie effect of it all for fear
we are watching the hungry dream of swallowing
the human race, the entire earth, dissolve
with the molten concrete and fragment glass
and atomized flesh, for fear horror will become truth
if we look away. And so the image repeats until it enters
our dreams: the recurring specter of the final retreat
to the same dust that birthed the poor as celluloid trickery,
a heathen lie somehow manifested in our captive light.
And the clichés line up like camels: *towel heads,*
swarthy nonbelievers, evil.

By some minimal trick of light, we are in the opulent city
and the name of God is our grieving and our waiting
for the deadly rain of thousand-pound bombs to turn the sinners
and the innocent in their strange hats to flaming dust
in the blink of an electronic eye, our loathing mirrored
back at us and, in turn, focused like a laser to flash point
and a peal of thunder to frighten God to tears, falling
now as impotent rain. The killers burning, the children
burning, the human race burning.

About the Author

MICHAEL MCIRVIN was born in the Nebraska Panhandle in 1956. He taught writing and literature for many years at various institutions, including Colorado State University and the University of Wyoming, and for the past several years he has been a freelance editor and writing mentor. His poems, stories, essays, and book reviews have appeared in hundreds of periodicals, and he is the author of nine books: poetry collections, novels, and an essay collection. He lives on the High Plains of Wyoming with his wife Sharon and is currently writing another novel.

Books by Michael McIrvin

Hearing Voices

Optimism Blues: Poems Selected and New

The Book of Allegory

Dog

Lessons of Radical Finitude

Love and Myth

The Blue Man Dreams the End of Time (novel)

Déjà vu and the Phone Sex Queen (novel)

Whither American Poetry (essays)